Scars to Stars

Email: dedrawaller@gmail.com

Facebook: www.facebook.com/iamdedra.com

Copyright © 2012, 2021 by Dedra Shanell Haynes-Waller

All rights reserved solely by the author. No part of this book may be reproduced, stored in a retrieval system, or transmitted in any form or by any means without expressed written permission of the author.

All content was provided to the publisher as original author work, not infringing on the copyrights of others.

Unless otherwise noted, scripture is taken from King James Version (KJV) Public Domain

As noted, scripture is taken from New Living Translation (NLT) *Holy Bible*, New Living Translation, copyright © 1996, 2004, 2015 by Tyndale House Foundation. Used by permission of Tyndale House Publishers, Inc., Carol Stream, Illinois 60188. All rights reserved.

Effective Date of Registration: August 31, 2012
Registration Number: TXu 001-823-197

ISBN: 978-1-62407-216-1
Printed in the U.S.A.

Scars to *Stars*

Dedra Haynes-Waller

Table of Contents

Acknowledgements ... 1
Foreword ... 3
Introduction ... 5
1 Sincerity ... 9
2 Sincerity of My Heart ... 19
3 Sincerity of My Heart, Part 2 ... 25
4 When You Just Don't Know What Else to Do ... 37
5 Consecration ... 47
6 Taking the Good with the Bad ... 57
7 Admiration ... 71
8 Restoration Then Salvation ... 79
Special Thanks ... 89
Thought for Today, Tomorrow, & Forever; Until You See Yourself Free ... 91
About the Author ... 93

Acknowledgments

First and foremost, I want to acknowledge the one and only true and living God - Father, Son, and Holy Ghost, for giving me this gift of language and teaching me how to use it. God has taught me how to take the good from the bad and use it to help others.

I am grateful to my husband Darryl, for encouraging me to write this book and to step out on faith in God. His push was what I needed to move forth in what I love to do, which is writing and helping others. Also, to my daughter and son, DaShana & Ra'keem, thank you for just helping in every way.

I am indebted to Kaye Manning and Donna Surber. They were my set of editing eyes. I am deeply thankful for Janice Carmicheal, Toni Fowler, and Zanetta Collins, whose friendship and wisdom have guided me through many uncertainties.

Most of all I thank my father and mother, George & Francine Haynes, for giving me life!

Scars to Stars

Foreword

I would like to introduce to you a wife, mother, aunt, sister, friend, and woman of God, Mrs. Dedra Haynes-Waller. Dedra was born on November 28, 1972, in Titusville, Florida. She is the daughter of George Jr. and Francine Haynes. Dedra, from kindergarten to first grade, spent time in South Carolina. Her family moved back to the Florida Space Coast permanently during the middle of her first-grade school year. Dedra found her talent for writing during her early childhood years, starting in the fourth grade. Dedra started writing poems and stories in private, not knowing at such a young age this would be the platform to bring healing to many.

Dedra graduated with both a Business Administration and Computer Science Degree, from Phillips Junior College in Melbourne, Florida in 1992 after transferring from Tampa College in Brandon, Florida in 1990. This transfer, although difficult, was a needed step in the completion of her degree, who many people thought she would not achieve. After working for others, Dedra became a licensed nail technician in 1995. She is the owner and operator of Nails by Dedra.

In her late teens and twenties, Dedra became the mother of two wonderful children, Dashana Waller and Rakeem Murray. After many years, Dedra and her high school sweetheart, Darryl Waller, Sr., rekindled their love and married. Dedra became the stepmother of four wonderful children. Darryl and Dedra's love was lost and found again through many ups and downs. They have been married since 2006 and look forward to the life journeys that are ahead.

During these years, Dedra continued to write. She filled many journals and binders. These writings were about the growth she gained through her life journey. Dedra discovered over the years that her foundation through life was anchored in God. Dedra continued to seek God throughout her young years and in her 30's discovered the love God had to offer was something she could not live without.

Dedra's thirst for knowledge has now allowed God to actively use her gift of prophecy, since June 2011. Through this anointing, Dedra now understands why she needed many stories and struggles. Through her writings she can touch others from a personal heart-driven place of knowing the pain; not just hearing of the pain.

This new author is sure to stir your soul, energize your body, liberate your mind, and heal your heart. The many who will embrace this author, will be intrigued by her knowledge and captivated by her strength. Mrs. Dedra Haynes-Waller; wife, mother, aunt, sister, friend, woman of God, and author, awaits your interest and love with great anticipation and respect, in the release of *Spoken Words from My Heart* and all other future releases.

This foreword was written with love and respect, from a friend that found her kindred sister. Dedra, you wrote this book through your fears and failures. For that, you have won, thrived, conquered, and survived. You have raised above it all. Now fly!

Love you always, baby sister!

Jasmine Pough

Scars to *Stars*

Introduction

It took me until I was almost forty years old to figure out this thing called *life's ups and downs*. Some scars and some stars.

All this time I'd been tangled up with *these* crazy thoughts and cares of this world. Thinking, because I was a female, my troubled mind was different than that of a male's. *Boy was I wrong!* Only difference was they just didn't know how to figure theirs out as fast as some of us women did.

Growing up in a little hick country town in Florida was quite an experience. Some of which I thought I could have done without, while the others made me wonder, how can one person experience so much in one's lifetime.

Yea, Lady D which was short for *Lady Dedra,* was my nickname and no one ever questioned why. I was glad. Glad because I would not have to explain where the name came from. One of my friends gave me that name while we were outside during P.E. class in middle school. Those days were some of the best days.

I've been told so many times, "You'll have to sometimes take the good with the bad and the bad with the good." How I wish that were only a myth. So, as you indulge in some of my life adventures, I pray that you are inspired to do something about the life challenges that sometimes tie you up from time to time. God will replace your hidden scars with His *scars*, equipping you for His Glory!

Selfishness	Sincerity
Cunning	Consecration
Addiction	Admiration
Repetitive	Restoration
Situations	Salvation

Included in this book are poems expressing my childhood experiences, teenage growing pains, and young adult life changes. When stepping into full on adulthood, I began experiencing a world of life changes on a day-to-day basis.

When your heart is free to express what it's feeling, the hurt, happiness, sadness, and grief, can become overwhelming. Many times, you wish they would just come and go away quickly.

Sincerity of someone's heart - the challenge is being real with yourself and expressing the different aspects of life's ever-changing obstacles.

Consecration by God allows us to be put in places where we don't always understand that it is Him molding us into the person we should be! It's only Him that can help us in our many difficult situations.

Admiration is the accolades you receive from others from doing ordinary insignificant things. It's almost how people admire you for the ordinary things that you do on a day-to-day basis. Often, it is the little things *you* take for granted; you're actually admired for.

Restoration is the act of being reestablished or rebuilt. When your dreams have been crushed, ideas stolen, and your self-esteem stomped on, God is more than able to restore you.

Salvation - Oh yeah! Salvation steps in; it comes as the saving grace of life. Thank God for His Salvation from our sins, and the assurance that He will carry us wherever grace leads us.

So often we gather information about others and think we know them. We often see their *glory*, but yet we are so far away from knowing their true *story*!

We are beaten up by difficult situations and many dysfunctional paths in life! We are backed up against a wall, with no one to really count on for lack of healthy relationships, sometimes even beginning to feel like the outcast of this world. We face obstacles daily, thinking they are life or death. Now take this journey with me and allow yourself to become free!

1
Sincerity

It was a long, long, boring hot day sitting in the house with no one to talk to and no phone in existence. I was looking out the window at Mama's house watching the neighborhood kids playing the Chinaberry game. If you were hit, you were out. This was a little pastime game we played. Take the berries and throw them at each other. The game didn't have teams, so when you were hit, you were simply out. Kind of like the dodgeball game we played at school, just without the ball, *ha-ha*. Seems boring in this day and time, but that was the number one game to play when you had a chance to play outside.

Everyone was enjoying the spring weather, the nice breeze, and having fun with one another. Hearing the neighbors next door be called in before the streetlights came on and watching them run like crazy to get in the house was always funny.

Mama is what we called my grandmother. Home cooked meals were one of the best parts of staying at her house. Mama had a way with those homemade biscuits and fried bologna. Watching her cook was like being in a candy store because you knew whatever you got out of it would be good. Everything had great flavor and taste, even the Kool-

Aid made you want seconds. *Man, those were the days!*

Good old *Uncle Bubba*. Uncle Bubba was my mother's brother whose real name was Woodrow Jr., named after my grandfather who passed away when I was five years old. I hold dear the memories of my grandfather coming in after work, as well as, the nickname he gave me, *Duck*. It was all I had to go on, along with what everyone else told me about him. My Aunt Neddie shared with us about her dad. She loved him so much. My grandfather was her hero!

Everyone called him Uncle Bubba and the name really fit him. He was our protector whenever we were staying over at his house. Uncle Bubba moved in with my grandmother shortly after the passing of my grandfather. He was a great help to my grandmother because she also had two other sons living there, both with disabilities: Charlie and Edward. Home away from home is what it was. Uncle Bubba was not only my uncle, but he was also my Godfather. We thought of him as our rescuer. All of us, his nieces and nephews, called on him quite often. Whenever we were in trouble with our parents for any reason he would protect us, making sure we didn't get a beating.

He would say, "Let them go with me! I'll straighten them out."

His way of *straightening us out* was for us to go in the house and sit down and taste some of the food he just cooked. He thought that was punishment for us, but we really were ready to eat. That was always a blast because he was a great cook! He would let us be in charge of answering the door, so if anyone came over, he could sleep without being bothered.

But, *oh boy*, on the other hand, when we were in a fight or argument with someone else or the kids in the neighborhood, all we had to do was mention his name. When someone heard us say, "I'm going to get my Uncle Bubba," they scattered. That was our favorite thing to holler in any difficult situation. Everyone in town knew Bubba didn't play.

I remember my cousin Tricia and I had gotten into a fight with some girls on 4th Avenue. We had beaten them good. They went and got their mother. She came to my grandmother's house right as we ran into the house.

It was always good that Mama made us keep on undershirts because we were running from the fight and pulling off the top shirts we had on. We were moving fast through the path trying to make it in the house before they got there. With our shirts changed, we thought she wouldn't recognize us.

As we ran by Uncle Bubba's car parked in the driveway, we were ecstatic because we knew if they came over, they would be in for a treat. They, of course, had no idea what kind of treat it would be. Uncle Bubba was home. She got there with her children, yelling and screaming in the yard. My cousin and I were laughing our heads off because they had no idea what they were in for.

Uncle Bubba hit that door. "Who in the hell do you think you are coming over here? These kids fight every day and yours got their butts whipped today. You need to leave before I get on yours."

Boy that was funny. Uncle Bubba was a big and tall man, 200 pounds easy with an attitude. They got out of there in a hurry. We laughed so hard our stomachs hurt.

He walked back in the house and found us on the floor laughing. He got onto us about fighting. Suddenly the laughing came to an abrupt halt. Then he told us that we better be glad we won, because if we had lost, he would have beat our butts for fighting anyway.

We loved him so much and we knew that he loved us too. Since he had no kids, all of his nieces and nephews were his heart. All our neighborhood friends knew he *really* didn't play. He was our *big dog* in the hood.

We shared many things with him and my grandmother. Since he and my grandmother were such wonderful cooks, it was hard to tell which one cooked the best. We enjoyed both of their cooking.

There were a lot of our family members with us in Titusville. We had our weekly Sunday meetings at Mama's house after church. We all staggered in one family after the other with our children for Sunday dinner and our family time. Straight in the door and to the patio for spades. If you had to wait and there weren't any seats on the outside, the next stop would be the den.

My Uncle Bubba didn't go to church, so while some of us were at church with my grandmother, he would stay at home and cook Sunday dinner. Some Sundays you would have thought they owned a grocery store after seeing all the food prepared on the tables. It was always enough for whomever stopped over, family or not. They both believed in feeding people. This was a family thing. Everyone, on both sides of my grandparents, liked to cook.

I remember my Aunt Heddie coming to visit on many occasions and cooking her favorite jelly cakes. She was my grandmother's sister. Whenever she was around her and Uncle Bubba had cook-offs, an easy way to gain five pounds.

Every time we were in the Carolinas, one way or the other, at every house surely there was something tasty to eat. Those were the good ol' days we now remember and cherish. We'd sit around laughing, talking, and eating. All of us; enjoying one another.

It was as if none of the other days mattered, whether good or bad, that moment in time was all that mattered! Just making it to Mama's house on

Sunday, was worth it. After going through *whatever* we encountered during the week, those thoughts were gone from our memory bank once we all got together.

Many of us had our differences. We were not perfect, but we all loved Mama and she didn't play with no foolishness in her house. She loved God and wanted all her family to love and know Him too.

Years passed and Mama and Uncle Bubba were gone. Mama had gotten sick. For a while she was sick off and on and had to go into a nursing home. I remember being at work and getting a call saying to hurry and get to the nursing home because she didn't have long left to live. That went on for about two weeks. Each time though, she made it through. Everyone was wondering and waiting to see who my grandmother was still holding on for. Suddenly we realized Uncle Bubba had not been to the nursing home to see her.

The last time they called the family up, Uncle Bubba went to see her. She died shortly after. No more pain or sickness. She was gone. Mama was the glue that held our family together. We knew things were sure to change and it did rapidly.

Uncle Bubba took her passing really bad. He just dedicated around thirty years of his life living with and taking care of Mama and my other two uncles. Next thing I knew Uncle Bubba had a massive stroke at work. They were both gone within three weeks of one another. I was much older by the time of their deaths, but the passing of them both so quickly added a little more fuel to this scarred heart of mine.

All this took place around Thanksgiving 1997. The hurt, disappointment, and grief were overwhelming at times. My grandmother's wake was on my twenty fifth birthday. Waking up on my birthday and knowing I had to attend her wake was so hard. I really was not sure I could do it.

Our family was already showing signs of falling apart. I knew this was something that had to be done. So, my birthday was just that - *another day*. Being so heartbroken, those two days were like a blur. Some things were clear, while others I don't even remember. I did not want that day to come and was ready for it to end.

The very next month, right before my son's third birthday on December 19th, Uncle Bubba's wake was held. That was a tough time for our family. In the blink of an eye, they were both gone from my grasp.

I remember the last conversation I had with Uncle Bubba. It was the night before his massive stroke. We were standing in the yard talking by the fence about how funny family was. I had no idea it would be our last time to laugh and talk. As I walked across the street to go home, we said our goodbyes. The next morning I got a call from Daphne saying,

Uncle Bubba was at work, but is now on his way to the hospital. He passed out and was nonresponsive. It was all downhill from there. The man I loved and cherished was sick and I could not do a thing.

Already having plans to go to Savannah, Georgia for the weekend, I decided to go for another visit to see Uncle Bubba before I left. He had the stroke on Monday. Going back and forth from Titusville to Orlando, I was told once the fluid drained, he would be okay. I went to visit him on Thursday. We had plans to leave out first thing Friday morning for Georgia. The last time I saw him, I talked to him, told him how much I loved him, and that I would see him when I got back.

The nurses said, "He can hear you." I knew he could hear me because, I saw the tears going down the side of his face as I talked to him. I also felt him move. The nurses said it was just a reflex but I still believe he knew I was there.

Early Friday morning we left for our weekend trip. While we were in Georgia, Uncle Bubba died. I was so hurt because when the phone call came through, hoping not to ruin our trip, my friends didn't tell me.

Well, I caught the next call that came through and was I upset! My life felt like it was in a serious earthquake with no sign of sunshine. Looking across the street and not being able to call on Uncle Bubba was going to be hurtful.

The day of his funeral came. It was so cold outside until the outside air felt still. I did not want to even go to the church and face this. I began to weep soberly, for I knew I would never see my uncle again.

As I walked in the family line up, I started to get dizzy; holding on to the pews, as I finally got into the church. I didn't want to be there. Lo and behold, all the pain I was enduring! My mind began to block what was going on. The next thing I knew, it was over. I had passed out and memories of the service were gone.

My heart was crushed, once again, for my dear uncle. He was gone from my touch. That was another piled-on scar. Seems like the hurt in my life had a way of just building up by the truck loads all of the time.

2

Sincerity of My Heart

My cousin Tricia lived with my grandmother and Uncle Bubba along with my other two uncles. I mentioned her earlier. She's like my sister, but we're first cousins. Tricia was raised by our grandmother.

I didn't ask questions, for we all have a story to tell. I knew she had hers, like I had mine. She always said, "I know it's for the best," and we left it just like that.

We shared many long conversations and late nights growing up; especially when everyone thought we had long been asleep. Our closeness started at a young age and carried with us onto adults!

Sincerity of the heart, we were what you would call the all-star phrase, *sister cousins*. Yes, truly indeed we were like two peas in a pod; like sisters - all those long talks and early morning mulberry pies we made. We actually learned what really went into those pies that made them worth eating: a lot of flour, effort, time, laughter, and sugar! Oh, how we loved making a mess in Mama's kitchen while she was asleep.

It's funny how growing up back then, and reflecting on how they now really teach us, makes us realize how important family really is. It was so important that some of us did get *it*, even if at times some others took it for granted.

Thinking back, every time I was at my grandma's house, Tricia and I spent a lot of time together, more than any of the other cousins. We were close in age which made it good. Having an older cousin, yet like a sister to me, was a great joy. She knew Mama like none of us other kids did. Her likes, dislikes, and especially when we got on her nerves. She would give us all the *dos and don'ts* whenever we came over. When to play asleep and when to run from Mama! That was always funny. We knew when she got that strap, it was time to be quite and quick or you were getting *it* if you didn't hush. Mama didn't play!

Those were growing-up days for a lot of us. I believe to this day, my cousin learned how to love and cherish people from living with our grandmother. She is now a well-respected nurse in our county. Over the years she cared for many people since the passing of Mama. Wouldn't you know, the elders are her favorite.

I used to wonder how she and I would turn out with all of the difficulties we endured as children. We shared so many similar feelings: being outcasts, feeling like loners, and wondering why there was hardly any closeness between our mothers and siblings. Even though I lived in the house with mine, we still shared those same feelings. I do believe God gave her a gift from Mama that she'll treasure forever, the gift of *compassion*.

We played a lot of games together and cried a lot of tears. We laughed and waited for the weekends. I remember the times we spent on 3rd Avenue. Few people knew how close we really were. Some probably figured it was because we were cousins; but we also had a close friendship. We did each other's hair and laughed at each other's silly jokes.

One of our favorite things was waiting for Saturday nights to come. We would try and play asleep while waiting to sneak outside. She stayed up and I would fall asleep. Then she would shake me and say, "Get up! We got to be nosey," or, "Oh no, someone's throwing a big party at Grey Coach End."

That was the town's grown folks club up the street from the *projects*. Standing in the corner of the yard at Mama's house, we could see the club down the street. Those corner lots kind of gave a glimpse of all that was around. The *old oak tree* on the corner of 3rd Avenue and Booker St. was the hot spot on Sunday evenings.

Mama's house was the place to be. All the families came over to laugh, eat, and play spades until nightfall. Those were the good ol' days when you could *see* the true meaning of the word family being shown. Like all things, times change and the ages don't remain the same.

As usual, it was time to go back to 208 Brown Avenue, where we lived. To our home; with fussing parents, distant siblings, and where everybody does their own things! My other uncle lived with his family right outside of our back door. A few steps more and you were in his house. Both our families grew up together.

People called where we live, *crosstown*. Most of our family lived on the other side of Garden Street, so our friends would say we lived *crosstown* from those that lived on the avenues. It was funny to them, especially when they knew we had to go home because we had no one else to play with *crosstown*.

We dreaded going home sometimes because we didn't have anything to do outside except ride bikes. Back then, things were a little rough for colored kids, just like it was for their parents. We lived in a good neighborhood but being the first two black families was a no-no in that *good* neighborhood. Mama's house was on the other side of Garden Street, *across town*.

I remember being almost chased down on my bike one day into our yard. I was in second grade. I rode my bike to the corner, to a little ice cream parlor called Cup and Cone. While on my way back home this man in his El Camino hollered out to me, "Little Miss Nigger."

He came at me in his car. I rode my bike as fast as I could, while screaming as loud as I could. I made it home grateful the ice cream parlor was just up the street. Into the yard I went just before his front end came up on the sidewalk. I jumped off my bike and started running. Good ol' dad, who was in the backyard cleaning fish, heard me screaming as I ran in the yard.

As my dad was coming out the front door, he saw the car speeding off and became very angry. He quickly went for his gun, but the car was gone.

Scarred! You do not even think at such a young age that *it* would stick and have an everlasting effect.

One day *it* showed up in school when I was in the sixth grade. We watched a movie called *Roots* all week. That Friday was a nightmare! After school, we walked down the pathway from Riverview Elementary School. Another student said, "I'm going to hang you like they did Kunta Kinte, Little Miss Nigger."

All I heard was *Little Miss Nigger*. Those words took me back to when I was chased by that man. Not thinking about school or the movie we just watched, I sent her on the ground and beat her butt. I got suspended from school for three days. I had unhealed scars that appeared later because they were not dealt with at the appropriate time.

So that's why we couldn't go outside in our neighborhood. It was too tough at home. It was freedom to get to the avenues. At my house, we would miss our favorite music playing and friends dancing at the park which was right up the street from Mama's house. The park's recreation center was where the action was. *The place to be*, right next to where we could go play games and get a drink of water, while watching the older teens play softball. That always was a blast.

But *crosstown*, at home, we didn't see any of that. Riding a bike or playing in front of the house was our entertainment. When my sister and cousin weren't hanging out with their friends, they would come in our bedroom and entertain us with their singing. They stayed home and entertained us because there was little else to do. Outside of that, it was just family time, work, and sleep.

Saturdays were fun because my dad would shine up his pretty candy apple 1962 Volvo or the 1974 green van or his 1974 green Charger and we would all go for a ride, ha-ha - *crosstown*. Even though some rides gave more enjoyment than others, time well spent with loved ones always made the ride worth taking.

3

Sincerity of My Heart, Part 2

As time passed, I moved right along, rapid changes in so many ways. My brother and sisters were just about grown and *oh boy*, we were really all different people.

My older sister from my dad, didn't live with us. She lived with her mom and other siblings. A lot of people said I could be her twin. She was a few years older than me, and I favored her a lot. Being the youngest of them all, I tended to see a lot more than *hoped* for.

Around the fourth grade I realized that writing was a natural and daily thing for me. By the eighth grade, I enjoyed writing so much, I knew in my ninth-grade year I was going to take a writing class as one of my high school electives.

Being so excited about going to the ninth grade, I had no idea I was about to face another challenge. I was with a cousin of mine at a hangout spot in Mims, FL, which is a little town north of Titusville. My whole world changed. I overheard her and another person debating on who was going to tell me something or *not* tell me what was going on.

"I'm not her sister," she said.

I got closer to see what was going on and asked, "Who is not your sister?"

My cousin blurted out, "She's talking about you!"

My mouth flew open. I knew she wasn't talking about me because I didn't know her. I never even saw her before. I guess since I was so cocky, it made her mad. The next words flew out of her mouth, "We got the same daddy!"

"What?" It was on from there.

Yes, she was my sister! I found out on an unused playground that the adults had taken over as their hangout spot. I wanted to strangle my dad for not telling me. I had a sister just six months older than me. I was mad!

My sister and me ended up talking. It was not our fault we did not know about one another; it was because of our parents. See, when adults hide so much stuff, the children suffer from it. From that day, I learned it is always best to tell the truth about one's affairs.

If you did it, face it, move on, and deal with it. If you are with someone who doesn't accept you and your past; the problem is not with them, it is with you. We all have a past. The truth is always better than a lie.

By this time, I was so ready for school to start. My writing teacher had no idea what she or he was in store for. I had a lot to get off my chest. I knew my homework and classwork would not be told to anyone other than my writing teacher. My hands were burning to get to a pen and paper.

At that time, I didn't realize those classes were a part of who I am today. After the first semester, I was told that writing counted as an English credit. Immediately, a smile radiated from my face. *Wow, no more dull English classes for me!* I was on the road to success. My outlet of pain was working in my favor.

Sincerity of the heart! When I was happy, sick, sad, or even disgusted, I had to put it into words. Those words began to release stress and built-up anger. Until this day, I had no idea what they really meant.

When I was a little girl, I can remember my grandmother, *Mama,* doing everything in her being to make sure her grandchildren had a little of everything she had to offer. She worked hard to teach us how important it was to love, share, and be a good person that others would be proud to look up to.

Hour after hour, while cooking, she'd sit us down to talk about her life stories as she remembered them. They were so interesting. When she spoke, we were unmovable, not wanting to miss a word. We didn't move because we were afraid of missing the really good part. These stories are some of what keep me striving to be my best.

Mama told us, "I worked hard to take care of my children and was always willing to help someone else in need along my way in life. You help people because you never know when you're going to be that person in need."

These words always bring pleasure to me, knowing that I can do more for someone when given a chance.

Let these words become a living thing in your soul. After being knocked down so many times and thriving to get back up again, we all need someone, at some place, or some point in time. Take charge and do what brings pleasure to your life. Life is a sure thing that you can't redo. So, we must try and do our best with what we have to make it better the first time around.

Dreams in the Storm!

Shadows appear in my dreams and again in a glimpse of the day
Soft voices and faint words no understanding of what they say
Hoping to see a face or to understand the whisper of that voice
Don't know what to do, to laugh, cry, or rejoice
How long must I wait to know the whisper or cry of the unknown?
Must I go left or right or remain all alone?
Waking up to a bright and sunny day
Helps smooth over some of the blankness that wanders my way
I haven't seen a face yet
though I feel someone's there as the wind strokes my face
Still waiting patiently, waiting for the order or my place
Is it that I've missed something without knowing when to look?
Or was it an imagination of a sob story along another brook?
So when you speak, please raise your voice a little if it's for me to hear
Soft, but kind would be appreciated or even thank you my dear
Blowing, blowing, gone by so fast
Hopefully this will come to surface
so this feeling of mine will become part of the past!

Dedra Haynes-Waller 3/16/2009

Scars, wow, how we try to cover them up with makeup and other things. Some come from more than being a different color. There are types of changes that dig deep down in your soul! Just to name a few:

- Having to take *stuff* from others, knowing they are wrong and the treatment given wasn't deserved.
- Feeling left out or mistreated for unknown reasons.
- Bad relationships.
- Being let down by those *thought* to love you.

Growing up in a neighborhood where blacks weren't made comfortable was bad and the damage it left was worse. Only about three families, in the whole neighborhood of twenty or more, would even talk to us.

There was a little church on the top of the street where they too welcomed us in. Thank God for Christians back then. It was rough growing up on Brown Avenue. My parents didn't really talk about racism too much. I guess it was too much of a sore subject. They would only say from time to time:

★★★ *Treat people how you want to be treated no matter the color of their skin.*

★★★ *Always remember that if someone does something to you that you can't handle, let them know.*

★★★ *Most of all, never let anyone disrespect you and you not speak up for yourself.*

All that being said was good, but how do you tell your parents that sometimes they were those people they warned you about? Some scars are so deep. They are there even when unseen on the surface. So deeply covered, you even forget how they got there because they have been covered up so tightly. Until years later, there's some pain you can't bear after trying to forget the nights, hour after hour, that caused such deep wounds in the first place, which were immediately covered up. You don't understand the agony of *this* feeling. You just know it's so intense.

There was pain, such screeching pain, from a wound that just wouldn't heal. *How could this go on for so long without healing? Why did it come up again? Where did it start and why didn't it truly end?* Covering it up at the time seemed to be the right thing to do, not understanding that the bandage would hinder the process of healing. I was lost without a clue. Not only was it covered, but it also began to grow. This thing had taken root in my soul from being buried so deep.

Changes in my life, that were sometimes misunderstood, have come from that *root*. Disappointing events, like being a part of a club and having no support or doing well in school and being told, *that's what you're supposed to do.* Crying for no apparent reason and feelings of being left out or never wanted came from this root. Scars that ran so deep under the surface of my daily walk came from this root. Scars without outward signs, unmasked hurts, and so many crushed dreams were a part of this root. Broken pieces that were never recovered in life and others that seemed to have went into the trash, still remain as fragments of my past, because of this root. Some thoughts were buried, others were shifted, and too many were wasted.

There are scars that no one wants to uncover, because they will uncover the hurting links of their life and those hurtful days, exposing so many others for their unlawful ways. Not realizing, keeping them wrapped embeds them in your soul. No one wants to feel what they felt before or deal with the inside of what's destroying the surface. When the inside is contaminated, it won't take long before the whole shell is destroyed. Once the shell is destroyed it takes almost a lifetime to reconstruct. Scattered pieces are all over the place. Some you can't even find under the trash and some fall in other places. Some are picked up by someone else and thrown into a bag. Some just fall at your feet; others you didn't even know you had.

> *Now you think things got to get better, but there is one piece that can't be found. It is lost in someone's bag of tricks and you're running out of time. Life stinks and you want to get past where you are before you lose your mind. There's this big black spot in your life that's yet unexplained but you're still too afraid to uncover what's close, especially since you don't want to endure any more pain. You continue to ignore the glare that gleams from under the shelf, painful nights and painful days. You turn to who was thought to be a friend or loved one and find out they are in the same boat you're in.*

I remember being thirteen, sitting by the window, watching the cars go by, and wondering: *Will someone ever stop that I could talk to or lean on, for just a little while, as a friend? Where in the world could they be going in such a hurry in this storm and rain?*

My friends were nowhere to be found. My family really didn't understand what was down in my heart. Shadows of my mind going rapid. Nothing is clear. *This can be so unfair! Is my soul being drained? Why do these pains haunt me day in and day out?*

Trying so hard to gain approval of so many people really did get tiring at times. Telling family and friends what they want to hear and hoping to be the favorite, while your self-esteem is torn down and carrying the weight of shame is draining. Enduring my parents' arguments about who spent the most money on me the last time and how much had to be given back, was crazy to me! I heard my father tell my mother, "I'll give you back the money you spent on her," or, "She's your child too!"

All this made me wonder, *Okay! Was I not both their daughter? What was the problem?* My mom seemed to do her share and that was that. My dad made sure he did his share as well. I loved them both and did not quite understand why I was the center of their argument. I wish I never heard any of it. Unfortunately, it became a family ritual.

As a little girl, I heard all that fussing and fighting while I was in my bedroom. It was something I always anticipated. I knew it was coming each day. I was sure to pay close attention to the words that were being said between the pauses of the argument. I was so sick of hearing, "She's your daughter, you do it."

Things thought only to be *nerve-racking* were doing a lot more damage than just racking nerves. I had no clue of what was going on most of the time. But I certainly knew that after a while of hearing that tone, it wasn't a good thing. It always came in at a bad time - in between an argument they were already having.

I am not saying they didn't love me, but as a child you think you're in the wrong or you did something wrong. No one's perfect. I'm sure there were reasons I didn't understand for those words to have come out.

As a juvenile or adolescent, you don't understand all the fussing over you, nevertheless, scars are being developed. You think you're not wanted.

There were some days that were nice and then others that were not so nice. Always hearing your parents argue, tends to cause you to draw near to the closest person that shows you love and attention. Drifting to another place, trying to get those thoughts out of your head, a poem comes to mind.

POPPING

Popping off like a soda cap on a hot summer day

One after the other nothing takes the thirst away

Taking one drink your body feels so fresh and cool

You forgot about water quenching your thirst,
    you drink like a fool

Only having sense to realize it would only take one cup

You've drunk a six pack and continue to screw up

Now exhausted with nothing by your side

You can't even get anyone to stop now that you need a ride

Walking down a path that's so familiar to you
    from way back when

Staring down a long road that has no end

Should you turn around because now you're hungry
    and need to eat

Still you don't know you've messed up a good thing
    that causes defeat

Do you stop and dig a hole in the ground and take a rest

Or do you continue to travel in the way of your mess

Darkness sat in and now you begin to worry,
    there's still nothing in sight

Where's your strength now, your strength at night

Soon you'll get a chance on another road of daylight again

Maybe next time you won't cheat at the game, just to win

4

When You Just Don't Know What Else to Do

My big brother was my safe place. He was my safety net, and he didn't even know it. My brother is about six years older than me. Growing up, I remember him being smooth with the girls and he thought he was the best thing walking. He loved sports and talking on the phone. Most of all, I knew he loved me.

Yes, he had a plan and I paid close attention to the steps he was taking. He was determined to go to school and make something of himself in life. When the *chips were down* and I couldn't get to Mama's house, he was the closest person for me to find comfort in. Even when he would kick me out of his room, it was still okay. I knew if he wouldn't let me back in, I could tell about his reports cards that were in a hole in his wall behind the bed.

When you're pushed all the time to the other parent, the other loses out. I guess as the years went on, that's how my dad and I became so close. I was labeled as a daddy's girl, but that is okay. So many people didn't know my story!

Growing up, we always had material things. Things weren't something we missed out on.

It's tough experiencing *tough love* as a child, rather than as an adult. I admired my brother for playing football because he had a way of escape from the drama. I wished I was the older one so I could leave first. I longed to be old enough to move out on my own. But being the youngest, at only 11 years old, where could I go?

Day to day was uncertain. I was scared of the fun times, because I didn't know if it was going to bring on a different outcome once the laughs were over. As adults we fail to realize some of our choices have lifelong effects on others. We are so accustomed to doing what we want, when we want, and especially treating others, children included, how we want.

We all do not have the same story, but most of us have shared some similar pain. If you have children, loved ones, or someone you know you have willingly hurt, ask God to forgive you. More importantly mean it from your heart, so that you may be able to be forgiven. If you have children, don't force them to deal with your adult insecurities when your life is not going the way you would have hoped. Above all, keep love in your home. It's never too late. God is a wonderful teacher. Thinking back, I wonder if the adversity I faced as a child caused me to dig deeper for the self-esteem needed to want more for myself as an adult.

My brother left to serve our country in the military right after he graduated high school. I prayed so hard for him to come back soon and get me. He was smart to have gotten out of this crazy house and town. *Wow, he has no clue that he was my hero.* If he could be someone good and do something good with his life after *this,* I knew so could I.

He never looked back from the moment he left. A year passed and I continued to think, he'd be back to get me. I always did my best, so I would be ready when he came to rescue me.

Next thing I knew, it was 1987. I was fourteen, awaiting my fifteenth birthday in a few months, and he was planning a wedding! *Marriage, a wife, wow, what was that going to mean for me? I would surely be lost!* I was hurt and confused wondering why he didn't want me. I thought maybe I should have told him I wanted to live with him in Germany. Still, I kept it to myself and kept quiet.

The wedding finally came. It was not what I'd imagined a good time would be. The sight and thought of the whole thing made me sick and sad. I knew in my heart that once he was married, I had no way of getting out of the hell house I was living in. Not every day was bad, but I thought it would be better if I could go off to Germany with my brother. Sad was an understatement. *What was I going to do?* My stomach had knots in it. I could hardly shake that feeling. What a combination to deal with!

I had a boyfriend at the time of the wedding but still wanted to move away. My boyfriend played sports and thought he had it going on. *Yes, so he thought!* He accompanied me to the wedding. Before I knew it, we were standing at the reception with my brother.

All my Godbrothers surrounded him and gave him the *low down* to not hurt me. Little did they know I was already hurt because my big brother had gotten hitched!

A few months later, a baby came on top of the marriage. *Okay.* At first, I was upset he had gotten married but the thought of being an auntie was nice. Although, all those dreams of me leaving were shattered. Trying to be happy all the time was hard, but I mustered up the strength from somewhere. Getting over it and just letting my brother be happy was a great choice, however I made it. I was fine with my choice.

I was acting like I had love for this boyfriend of mine. I thought I was feeling what my brother was feeling. *It's on now*, or so I thought! Boy was I wrong and at the wrong age. The boy was a cheater and had several girlfriends. I wasn't his only one. *Oh no, this was starting to be a nightmare all over again. Wow, was I young and naïve?*

At school, I took his folders out of his backpack and ripped them up piece by piece to shred every girl's name I saw written on them. Yes, sounds crazy. I was hurt and I took pleasure seeing him sweat because he thought he was a player. I was *green* and didn't know the streets. I didn't think he had another girl. Wrong! He was as spoiled as spoiled could be. He drove his own car way before I knew him. *What do you do? Make it easy or make it hard?* Oh yeah, he was making it hard. He thought he was the only smart one all the time. *High school boyfriend, what was I thinking?* Athlete and fine are two things that don't mix in high school, unless you are a Christian 😊.

It can be difficult at times thinking we have someone who *finally* loves us. Surely, we think we've found our soulmate the first time they say I love you. But try to be mindful, the hurt is sure to come when you start second guessing so many of a person's actions. Ask questions. If not to them; *shucks*, at least to yourself. *Do I really know them, or do they even know me?*

Hurt has its way of becoming a stronghold. If you're not strong enough, that stronghold will take a big hold of you. I was hurt by so many people, especially those so-called boyfriends in high school. I decided to hurt them back. Hurt wasn't a stranger to me. I had gotten used to it. I decided not to take anymore crap from anyone who wasn't going to be honest with me, whether in high school or not. It is an understatement to say the two experiences I had in high school with cheating football player boyfriends were bad. *More scars.*

For too long, I allowed others to take the *good* of who I knew I was and trample on it. Not aware of how much damage was being done, I continued to hold onto that hurt. I was even used to my family sucking the good out of me, to the point of no longer recognizing some of the *tricks* that came from others. The so-called friends seemed better sometimes than some of the on and off again family members.

Grabbing as much as I could of the self-worth I had left, I found myself fighting to get back on some type of good track. Anything had to be better than what became *my usual*. Even when I didn't understand what was going on, I knew there had to be something better for me. I was determined to get it no matter what. I was searching for something better than those rough times:

> *Now I see the beginning and the end, with not one punctuation at all! Help me figure out what You are saying God. Please don't let my world fall. Help me to regain what You have given me to share with Your people. Please don't let my thoughts cloud Your direction for me. Keep my mind so that I may serve You in spirit and truth in everything that I write.*

As a young child I remember how the other kids always had free time for their summers. I was the only child of my dad's from my mother. My siblings had their own father from my mom's previous marriage. So, I was the only one always sent to South Carolina to spend my summers with my paternal grandparents. Crying sometimes to the point my eyes hurt, I was left with no one there to play with except for my grandparents. Not that I didn't love them, but because I was so far away from home, it was hard for me. I was only five years old.

I didn't quite understand at first why it made me so sad, but it did. Waking up each day and knowing I had no way to get home was always terrifying. I had to deal with the fact that I was a child with no choices.

I can remember my grandfather cutting up cucumbers and tomatoes for me. Trying to cheer me up, he would say, "Come on baby girl, put the salt and pepper on it."

That was big for me. I imagine he was the friend I needed. My grandma would bake cakes and cookies, also making me feel better, to take my mind off of my siblings not being there. My dad always told her to make sure I went to see and feed the pigs. That was fun too. I didn't take any of this for granted yet I asked myself, *why was I chosen to be so different?* I harbored those times as bad times, until I decided to forgive my parents.

I had gotten used to going to South Carolina for the summers. Grandpa, who had become a friend, passed away. *Why was I going through so much loss and now another grandfather was gone out of my life? More scars!*

Meanwhile I was getting older, finally old enough to go to my mother's hometown, Andrews, South Carolina for the summer. The destination was my uncle's house. My uncle Robert Lee and his family would let us kids come and spend the summers with his kids while our parents stayed in Florida and worked. That did make me feel a little better. Now I was able to go somewhere else for my summers, other than St. George.

    I was doing what I was told. My uncle would let me go uptown to visit my other cousins who came up from Miami to stay at their grandmother's house. Ol' Aunt Wilma, yes, her house was the place to be. Stephanie, Shante, Angie, and I became really close while spending time in Andrews each summer. We are still close to this day. When we went places up there, people thought we all were sisters. We let them think that so they wouldn't ask us a lot of questions.

    We learned a lot staying in the country and now we can take those things we learned and cherish them. The things we experienced back then, we probably would not have, if we weren't made to go up there for summer break.

    On Sundays we all would go to Aunt Della's house to see her and her family. Sometimes during the week, my uncle would switch it up and let me go to Aunt Della's house to spend time there. I loved being there because her daughters would spoil me. My cousin Chris and I were kind of close too. I had finally started really enjoying my summers. The thought of having to come back to Florida was always tough!

Then the teenage years kicked in. Everyone started staying home. The summer visits were over! Back to reality once more.

5
Consecration

Consecration becomes a part of us even when we don't know God is molding our lives from scars to stars. In the midst of this consecration, my life became hard work with many difficult tasks and trials.

My mind goes back to the summer before my tenth-grade year. I wanted to be a part of our high school girls varsity basketball team. I realized I wouldn't have any support because Mom and Dad weren't into sports.

My mother had been torn apart after my brother's chin accident when he played football years back. It made for a long night. He had a football game, but we didn't go. I heard my mother scream as she got the phone call telling her he was hurt. He had to go to the hospital to get stitches in his chin. It was over from there for the sports. So, from that point on sports were a sore spot for her. My dad, well, he just wasn't a fan of sports other than watching wrestling in front of the TV set on Monday nights.

How do I go home and say, "I want to really do this and be on the team?" Taking the chance of it being okay or not, was a thing I was ready to deal with. I began going to the practices and made it through tryouts. I made the team, but the team didn't make me. *What does that mean?* I wasn't going to change from who I was like some of the other girls did. I just wanted to play ball.

Everyone had to take a physical so that included me. I went to the doctor's office to get my physical. I was nervous. After the physical and before the doctor called my mother in, he said to me, "Do you have the nerve to tell your mom or would you like me to?"

Me being a smart butt thought: *You can tell her what you want. I'm playing basketball because I already made the team!*

He asked again, "Do you want me to tell her?"

I responded out loud this time, "Sure, she knows I want to play basketball. Sure, tell her. I'm okay."

His reply was, "Not only are you okay, you're pregnant!"

My mouth flew open. I think my heart went to the floor along with my attitude, "Pregnant?"

"Yes," was his answer, "so would you like for me to tell her?"

I was so scared. At the same time, I felt she can't kill me in front of the doctor so that made me feel a little better. My thoughts quickly shifted to what our ride home in the car would be like. I began to sob again.

Yes, I was pregnant. I was not going to be playing basketball. Just that fast, my season began and ended, all in one week. Nevertheless, I didn't know what I just experienced would be the next event to drastically change my life.

Lots of tears and nine months later, came a special little girl. Not only did the fact that I was a young mother change my attitude, but it also changed my life. I had to get a job early. No more just going out *because*. I had to think about taking care of my baby.

I had no plans of going to college. That changed the moment I found out how much it cost to take care of a child. All the plans I thought I had of becoming a writer or a model were over. The modeling career was especially done because my body changed. I looked like I swallowed a big ball.

I continued high school and started a job at a nearby restaurant. My boyfriend and I took turns working and taking care of our baby girl. I worked at a seafood restaurant. He worked at a local grocery store. Graduating high school, a year early, at the age of sixteen with my ten-month-old baby girl, was an experience I will cherish forever. I made plans to go to Tampa for college.

Right before going to college, I experienced a lot of not so good trials in my life. My best friend Deborah and I, had big dreams of getting away and making our lives better for our children. We both were involved in not so good relationships and needed a change. I was dating this guy who just had to have every woman in his sight. I named him "Mr. Cheater." Deborah and I would laugh about it all the time. Men like that thought they were invisible and no one knew they were dogs.

    We moved to Tampa and started school. She had her baby, and I had my daughter along with my eight-year-old niece Shekita. Yes, I was raising my niece while trying to go to college and take care of my daughter. It was a task at first, but she was a great help. God allowed me to help her in her situation and she was helping me too. My daughter had someone to be with her while I did my homework. What looked like a bad and hopeless situation turned out to be a blessing! My niece was now like my own little girl.

    Some days I cried, wondering how I could take care of two children, when I was only seventeen going on eighteen and in college. I started questioning God. *Was graduating early from high school a good thing?* After I got over my pity party, I realized someone had to do it. My sister couldn't, my mom was tired, and my niece needed me. We made it through!

    After moving back to Titusville another journey began for us all. She was with me for a few years before she encountered her own set of scars which also added to mine. I thought surely it was enough to ruin both our lives, yet God had another plan. I knew one way or the other, at that point in life, I surely had to get out of what I was in, not only to be a positive example to my own daughter, but to her as well.

It was time to do something about the relationship I was in and my life in general. Even though I was experiencing such tough times; I was so ever grateful for all the friends I did have. They were there for me when I thought I couldn't get up out of the rut I was in.

Time continued to tick and go by so fast! The relationship was challenging, but I got through it and it was over. I was so upset for allowing myself to even go there with him because he lied to me about still seeing another woman. Since I had went off to school, he got married to get back at me! *What a big no-no! This whole thing was just plain out wrong! What was I thinking? Why did I allow myself to stay involved with such an overload of problems?*

All in all, I had a mess on my hands and was glad to be rid of it. Not only did I have an encounter with "Mr. Cheater," but there was also "Mr. You Don't Even Go There," and "Mr. Do Wrong." *Scars, sure enough!*

I didn't know how wrong it was until I had went and came back from college. I began to discover who and what I had gotten myself into. Dealing with the fact, I had run into a not so good relationship again, dredged up old scars from my high school days.

Along came the deep, double deep, lashes of adult cutting scars. The kind that cut, not only the surface, but hit and tamper with some spots of your soul. *Talk about deep wounds!* Some of which I tried for years to keep bandaged, not knowing I was hurting myself by not dealing with them. I watched so many of my friends experience hard relationships. To find myself almost in the same boat was crazy. Scars began to pile up, one on top of the other. I didn't know what to do!

Not only was I in a relationship of heartache, but I was pregnant again. Trying to manage an up and down relationship, while expecting a baby, is complicated. Well, lo and behold, I lost the baby. There I was initially, not really wanting to be pregnant under the circumstances I was in, but I eventually faced the fact that I was pregnant, and I was preparing to have my baby.

In the winter of December 1992, I was due to deliver. Of course, they told me it could be two weeks give or take. Well, on the twenty-eight I just knew I was going to have the baby, but they sent me home. After going to my doctor, the next week for a checkup, he informed me, "If you don't have this baby by the twelfth of January, I'm taking it."

I was excited to have a clear timeframe for my baby's arrival. I went in for my check up on

January twelfth and was let down, because he extended the date of delivery to January twenty-fifth.

It was a long, long day on the nineteenth of January 1993. I woke up happy, with plans to go to the Martin Luther King Parade. I was fat but I thought I was pretty. After breakfast I was ready! I went to the parade and ate so much. I thought the baby was full because he was moving really slow all day. About six o'clock, I decided to go to the emergency room, because I could hardly feel any movement.

My mother said, "Before you go, call and ask to talk to a nurse."

I did and I explained to her what I was experiencing. She suggested I eat something sweet and then if there is no movement after an hour to come in. I was listening and eating at the same time. I waited for about fifteen minutes, and I left for the hospital.

One of the saddest days, of my life! The baby's heartbeat was faint on the monitor. They made me wait for two more hours to have a sonogram done. By the time the doctor finally called to tell them what to do next, my baby's heartbeat was gone. I was left feeling like my world was about to end.

I had support with me at the hospital; seems like everyone I knew was there. My first thought was, *why am I being punished even more?* Days later, I had to not only give my son a name, but to have his funeral as well. I was lost for months and didn't really know how to make a comeback. *Deeper scars!* At age twenty-one, it felt like I was twirling in some type of case of bad luck.

    I had a lot of support and finally found my way back to reality, but the process was more than I understood. Yet the reality of it was another scar that I covered up. I was so hurt. Some mornings my heart hurt so much. It felt as if my entire body was submerged in needles every time my feet hit the floor.

    Still moving the best way that I knew how, I became a nail tech, which helped me more than words can say.

    My best friend Deborah was a saving grace for me. Every day she made sure I was okay. We both worked at the Space Center, and to my surprise she took a leave of absence just for me. Every day she made sure I ate and had someone to talk to. I stayed in the house for a few months. I only went out to go to doctor's appointments. Deborah never left me without calling back.

    One day she said, "You're always painting your nails and trying to do your own with acrylic nails, do mine!"

    So I did! They looked a mess, yet she never complained. She just sat there for hours and let me pile all that acrylic on her nails knowing that they were ugly. After those few months at home with

Deborah, I had acrylic nails down pat. I was so grateful for every kind and honest word she imparted into my life. Words could never express how she was a blessing to me. She was my first real customer and friend.

Two years later, I registered for Brevard Community College's nail technician program. Decades later, to this day, I'm still a licensed nail tech.

Once I was able to get around other people and help them feel good about themselves, I knew the nail tech job was a gift from God. It was also helpful for me. I always had someone around me to talk to.

God sent people my way to encourage and help me through a difficult time in my life. I had no clue at that time where I was even going with my life.

I prayed every day that God would free me from this life of so much pain. I felt I needed a *grace and mercy break*. Later, I did feel some relief. Time passed and things became better for me. My relationship was on the right track, and I found myself moving forward!

While moving forward, I got pregnant again! I wasn't for sure I even wanted to have any more children after the stressful ordeal I just came out of. I prayed God would have mercy on me. My life was at another crossroad. The months passed so quickly, and everything was fine with me and the baby.

In the month of December, on the twenty-first day of 1994, I gave birth to a bouncing baby boy. *Who would have thought that something good would finally come from such a bad relationship?*

Before I knew it, God had worked that thing out. After almost fifteen years of being in a whirl wind of a relationship, it was over! I had my two kids and we were on the path to getting on with our lives.

6

Taking the Good with the Bad

Speaking of being in a time of consecration - taking the good with the bad, was an understatement!

These times are for molding and teaching, even when we don't know what's really going on. Our minds are being transformed. Often, we try to hold on to a place of comfort or safety, not realizing the work of God is at hand. A special purpose or service is yet to come.

Wow! Even at this time in your life God can be setting you aside for His purpose without you knowing that it is a part of His will for your life. First, He considers the source. Then He prepares the table and begins the order of processing you. For His glory!

I can remember during trying times in my life, wondering *why* and *how* I got the privilege of having so many hard times and heartaches. Going through high school was bad. Of course, we all have friends that come and go, but some things I could have done without.

I had chosen to go back to school, which was a good thing. It was hard at first leaving my daughter with someone else, but I had to do what was best for us. I was in a monumental moment in the consecration process.

Looking back, in hindsight, we can see the paths that were chosen for us without us having a say in the matter. *O yes, that was a time of consecration.* There are times God automatically places us in a situation, where we can't say or do a thing. Whether we *think* we deserve it or not; it's not always our choice to make.

> *Maybe this was one of the roads you began to travel although you clearly heard a Voice in your ear say, "turn right," but you continued to go your own way.*
>
> *After following the pathway you chose, you ran into a dead end. Most of us have experienced dead end difficult relationships. That stalker, yes, he turned out to be no good at all. Or the afternoon drunk that wouldn't get off the couch and get a real job. My God, not to mention the player, player of the town, the big time "wanna be" with four and five women he calls his ladies, yet he has nothing in mind for a real future. Then there's the man that leaves a baby after every relationship he has and still ends up in your bed at the cost of your emotions.*

Scars to Stars

Oh yeah, that's sure enough a bumpy road you had to wean yourself off. After the hits upside your head and the long afternoon cries, you wondered, "Was I really supposed to go to the stop sign or turn before the road ended? If so, I made the wrong decision and it cost me. Now I'm in this place, with him."

So many uncertainties! Meandering around with lost hopes and unfulfilled dreams, you're looking for help to just figure this thing out, but no one or nothing comes to mind. You're in the wilderness wanting to get out but you don't have the strength. Consecration is more than some of us ever bargained for.

With prayers you wish you could be twenty-one again so you wouldn't feel the full effect of this great adulthood that awaits you at the age of twenty-five and over. Hanging out on a Friday night with your close friends or playing spades until it's time to go to the club or to bed, finding yourself passed out on a Saturday morning with a hangover, or worse with someone else's girl or boyfriend are all what we thought were the times that brought us to new levels of maturity. We didn't take into consideration that those days would come to an end sooner than later. Mortgage, rent, electric, water, and insurance would be the next boyfriend or girlfriend in your life. In the back of your mind you think, where would Mom or Dad be, how much of this would either of them play a part in? Then you realize the reality is, although they may have played a part in your life earlier on, now it's your show time - adult life.

All the times we took for granted that our past days would be our best days, are gone. I was still being consecrated, without missing a beat of life's challenges along the way! Even my thoughts started to disappear.

After reading a book on my shelf called, "Help I'm Raising My Kids Alone," by T D Jakes, I realized I had experienced what was called *writer's block*. I didn't even know that the very thing I loved was stuck right in front of me with no place to go. My mind, heart, and soul longed for a pen and paper to continue, yet nothing came. Being in so much heartache and pain from physical use of this body, I had undergone a blockage unknown.

My world, on a daily basis, had become crowded. I needed comfort, deliverance, and shelter. Most of the time, I only had a little peace and that was when I was in prayer and with other saints. The overflow was always great, only to be sucked out by the cares of this world.

Scars to Stars

When we lose focus on the greater things for the small things of the past, they seem to look larger than they really are. The scars of my life were actually bothering me more than I could ever imagine. I didn't know how deep they had gotten. Trying to uncover why there was always hurt, with only little relief, was starting to get old.

The past really wasn't the thing of the past. It still lingered. The scars I thought were hidden weren't healed. They had just been covered up for so long. It was like wanting a new bandage and not being able to find one that fits comfortably because they all made the wound hurt more. Letting *it* get fresh air, knowing *this or that* would help, and trying to forget the pain only lasted for a little while.

Difficult times continually coming downstream, at such a fast pace, seem so unreal. As I sat and talked to my close friend Sam, she told me about a troublesome time she had. As she spoke about a horrible time she'd never gotten over, my mind went back to a scarring time in my own life, rewinding back to a night of endless fear from being locked in a room. I kept thinking there's no way out, yet I continued to pray someone would come to my rescue soon to liberate me. As I laid on the cold hard floor, I prayed God would get me out of the mess I had gotten myself into; unsure if my so-called boyfriend would really return to finish me off.

He always had an attitude and threatened to take my life if I ever left him. Running away from the horrible hits to the face, I just wanted out! Those nasty beatings became unbearable, yet the scars were continually covered up. I found myself hiding back tears in public places when asked how things were going.

Is your mind plagued by questions of uncertainty? How did you get here? When will it end? Why, why do you stay? Constantly waking up, with a beautiful face and broken heart – why is this the way you start the day? Low self-esteem is hidden within a very smart person; trapped for the moment. Broken, but not broken-down. Shaken, but yet unmovable. You start to regain your strength. You pick up the pieces that were chipped around the edges. You begin to put yourself back together again, not even knowing how.

This consecration has been working in your favor. The heartaches don't seem to hurt as much or seem as bad anymore. Your hair that was lost from all the stress begins to grow again. You feel better about your appearance. Now you can go back to Finally You Salon and get your hair done! Yes, God is moving things around. To your surprise, you can finally get a job. Yes, yes, yes things are looking up. The one person who was bringing you to your knees with teary eyes is now no more. Thank you, God! Getting it back and taking it back; everything that was taken from you starts to return.

Although everything was moving slowly, it is now moving in your favor. The job, the kids, and the pets begin to look like new life. No more two-timing men in your life. No more fly-by-day friends. You enter into cruise control as a newly molded you.

Step back and let me through, you think to yourself, as you enter a crowded room of spectators who once watched your life flip flop you daily. Stand aside; it's still me, just newly improved by grace. Eyes cannot seem to come off your beautiful dress as you sashay across the room. All eyes are on you. The time spent in turmoil doesn't seem so bad after all. Once you step like no one could, you know you are on your way to bigger and better things. Yes, the players even know not to approach you. Backup!

I just didn't want to have any of *that* on my hands anymore. But before I knew it, the wounds presented themselves again, one way or the other. It was not getting better. Covered up and yet too revealing, is how a hurtful past torments people from day-to-day when the healing process has not taken place. The scar is always there to remind us of what needs to be tended to, but too often we let it go unattended. We tend to avoid the initial pain of what is really underneath and deep down on the inside.

For years, I wondered *how* and *why* I was so different from my siblings. As time went on, all of what I tried to cover up, God uncovered when my life was at the point of readiness! Maturity is a great factor. Being young and immature only adds to the pain and makes more or bigger scars. *Who wanted to endure that again? Not me!*

So, as I grew, things began to unravel inside and outside of me. So many endless thoughts traveled through my mind that had hardly any meaning. *How do these thoughts connect? How do I describe what I'm feeling? Is this a sign? Can things really change this quickly before my eyes? Is it that I haven't taken the time to try and figure out what the words really are saying to me? Have I lost what I had been longing for? What am I supposed to see?*

Drifting all over the place, the words came faster than ever, one after the other without a place to jot them down. It's as if our minds make us think one thing, but the facts are completely the opposite.

I am reminded of a story. A young lady thought she had the man of her dreams. *Oh yeah, he was a hit.* Muscular, brown eyes, the smoothest conversation you could imagine, dressed to a tee, and haircut by Titusville's finest barber Mr. Linc. He opened all the doors, made breakfast, and even watched her while she swam laps in the pool. *Sheep in wolves clothing!*

Her best friends thought very highly of him, until one day he left his coat at her place. It was a cold and rainy evening. While he was at work, she thought she would return his coat by just leaving it in his car without disturbing him since he was on the job. She knew the door would be open because he was always afraid of locking his keys in the car. Once the rain slowed, she thought now was the time to surprise him and take it over.

Opening the door, she sat the coat on the seat. *Wow, she thought, he's bringing me flowers. Now what do I do? Do I take the coat back so that I don't ruin the surprise?* Hurrying away, she left the parking lot hoping not to be noticed by anyone.

Hours passed and it was time for him to come by or at least call. The weather had picked up and it was now even colder. She was expecting him sooner than later.

After waking up from an unexpected nap, there was no phone call missed nor any knocks at the door. *What happened, did I miss something?*

Two days passed; no sign of him. Mr. Special wasn't turning out to be Mr. Special anymore. Not less than two months into the relationship and it was beginning to show that he was just another one of *those* guys.

He finally called after day three and began with a long-drawn-out work history story. *Blah-blah-blah,* is what she thought. There was no need to even mention the flowers she had seen. She just listened to the lie and kept silent.

A few more months passed, again a night of passion. He left to go for champagne and calls back, "Hello, hey honey, I've gotten a call, have to make a quick stop, and I'm on my way."

Of course. Hours pass before he walks back through the bedroom door. She's not even interested anymore. She lays there silent, pretending to be asleep. She thought, this is getting to be a problem of which she isn't going to deal with anymore.

Suddenly, *ring-ring,* it's the doorbell! Since she is pretending to be asleep, she can't move. *Who could that be at 2:30 in the morning?* The rings changed to knocks. The knocks escalated to bangs. Okay, now she's up, and asks, "Honey could you see who that is at this time of morning?"

Now, you all can think back, like she did, to the flowers that were in the car and the sudden lack of phone calls. She opened the door anxious to know who was on the other side. Standing there, as the door flew open, was a woman wearing the exact same nightgown as she had on.

"Yes! Can I help you?" she asked.

The response came quick. In a loud voice the other woman exclaimed, "As a matter of fact, you can. You can send my husband out!"

She was so stunned seeing the lady standing there in the same type of nightgown he had bought her. Her response was slow. The woman spoke again, "Could you tell my husband I'm here?"

Wow! Husband! After hearing both voices, he disappeared. He was really a *special* kind of guy; one of *those* guys.

See, we fail as people when we don't get all the necessary information on someone. The signs are there but we ignore them for the sake of *Mister or Miss Do Right*. They come along with those sweet words. We're all in love and in la-la land. They're in our beds, with no thought; and then we're all a mess after they leave. All of this is what makes us become victims of scarred relationships. We must recognize the *bumps in the road* as a sign to slow down, proceed with caution, or take another road. When we ignore the signs and lose our way, we end up having to go through a longer consecration process.

> *You find yourself wanting to just be taken out of this point of despair you're in. Another episode hits you.*
>
> *Now your finances are all blundered up because you just had to buy the new suit or get a new car. Maybe you just felt like*

gambling and thought you'd win. Nope! Tables turned and you're now in a jam. What is there for you to do now? Mama, Daddy, no one can help.

Now you're back to being molded a little more. You thought you were past this point, but here comes more pressure reforming you.

Lo and behold, a change is beginning in your life. Things don't look so bad after all. You begin to make better choices. You've started to see the sunshine a little more and then here comes something else. Are you going to fold? What are you going to do now?

That feeling of torment, from being in that marriage with that cheating husband, arises again. The pain from the liars on your job, and not to mention, the hypocrites who sat with you along the pews at church every Sunday, are causing you more stress.

Your mind goes crazy once more. It's something to experience hurt in the church, the very place you should find comfort. The overflow actually started to spill over like sour milk. What is the use of going to church when the same things going on outside the building are going on inside the building?

Scars to Stars

Discouragement. You know it shouldn't be that way. You saw things differently while growing up; yet you're so tied up and tangled up in your own sin, you begin to question yourself. Why are you even there? No place to just ask for help. You just travel through this hurtful maze of life.

7
Admiration

Admiration, in hope, carries us from day to day. The spoken word comes through like pure gold. The writing on the wall looks clearer with every glance. The grass even looks greener when the fog has lifted out of your eyes.

> *Unknown gifts shower your days and nights, flooding you for unknown reasons. Thank yous are flying from everywhere, even from those whom you never expected, along with surprises of warm heartfelt hugs and kisses! Refreshing thoughts are dancing around in your mind, "What did I do to deserve this honor? When did I become so loved and why did I not see this before?"*

> *People who look up to you with great respect, have entered your surroundings, offering helping hands and favors. It's like a man with many servants, waiting on your every move. You know it's not true, but your heart feels like you're on top of the world. What a good feeling to be admired in such a pleasant way, even to the point of being overwhelmed.*

You open the door at a restaurant and feel like everyone is smiling at you, even though they don't really know you exist. You see the millionaires all drooling to the sound of your pumps tapping the floor with every step you take. The music plays to the beat of your walk, as if the song was written just for you. Not planning on staying for this big event, only an appearance is what you wanted, you exit the party after about thirty minutes.

Life is back on task and in motion. Like new wine, is how you now feel. No time to think back on shallow dreams or negative conversations because you're off to a brand-new start. New friends are what your lips softly utter after you breathe a quiet, "Wow."

You remember those days when you felt like just giving up. Then suddenly, when all else had failed, God gave you strength to go on, just to bring you to this present time in your life right now. You are transformed, and being further transformed, from one person to someone greater. You use your past to empower your great future. The strength that comes from others' love, helped you make it through those tough and not so happy days. You become okay!

Working towards something that brings pleasure in life feels wonderful. It's rewarding to get back to family who witnessed the hard times we encounter, yet later see our life change for the best. Being welcomed with open arms, makes it worthwhile to be in their presence. This is worth living for, worth making a new day and a fresh start.

Thoughts of *why, how*, and *when* occasionally drift through our minds. *Why didn't I see this before? How did I allow myself to be taken under by this and when did it first grab a hold of me?* Believe me, thanks to God, it had now begun to look better.

Things were once more, finally, starting to look like life was worth living. Some tasks were still challenging, but others were like small hills that I could just roll over.

Being in one place for so long, can cripple one's ability sometimes to strive for more. Our mind tells us to *hold on to what we know, then we will be okay.* Not realizing, that state of mind is a limitation. We must know, we are capable of picking up one foot after another, and each time we do, we move to a place we haven't been.

This reminds me of a story that I know all too well from my childhood. Going into adulthood, I thought all a person had to do was come to grips with where they were in life and ask God for guidance to help them walk through the next open door. Once we ask Him, I thought the next step was simply to watch

Him move any obstacles out of our way. As I lived some more, I learned that gaining knowledge of what gifts we have and our reason for being on the earth, is what brings our life together. The realization that the time of consecration was well worth it, comes with maturity.

Lo and behold, I am here with gratitude to open the window of true love for you to step in, into a new time zone, and new day.

> *"Life's worth living," the voice in your head is screaming out! People can now see you in a different light than before. No longer walking in darkness of despair, you feel free.*

It's so important that we try to deal with our hurts when they are on the surface, because once they start to seep in, they are hard to dig out. When we encounter so much pain from others, they may forget, while we hold on to those scars. I've been around people who've had hurtful things said to them and they just kept silent. *Remember, no more!* You must take a stand for something, so you do not fall for anything. Life is too short to always be miserable.

- ★★★ *It's time to take back your pride that was stolen when you were on drugs.*
- ★★★ *It's time to take back your self-respect that was compromised when you were raped.*

Scars to Stars

- ★★★ *It's time to take back your self-esteem that was depleted every time they laughed at you for being heavier than your peers.*

- ★★★ *It's time to take back your dignity that was discarded while on alcohol or drugs.*

- ★★★ *It's time to take back your self-worth after a horrible marriage, in which your spouse thought it was okay to misuse your love. Oh yeah snatch that one back!*

- ★★★ *Then just lean over and grab all of your joy that you missed when your so-called friends weren't who you thought they were.*

- ★★★ *Now that you're on a roll of being restored, don't forget to pick up your happiness along the way that was robbed at gun point because you chose to speak up for what's right.*

- ★★★ *Get restitution for everything your family members picked your pockets for. You know the ones who know it all.*

- ★★★ *Block the mumbo jumbo of "hey only men make babies, not boys," even though it's the women who have them and sometimes raise them on their own. That has been the story for centuries.*

- ★★★ *It's time to know that all things happen for a reason and season.*

★★★ *While in your season, do what God gives you the strength and allows you to do. For it could be worse. Just thank that person for whatever contribution they have given for your being here. If it had not been for your donor, you would not exist.*

★★★ *Let those scars encourage you to be a better parent than you had. Yes, they were equipped to make you and have you; they just weren't equipped to nurture you. Not having two parents in your household, doesn't mean that your absent parent doesn't love you. Nor does that mean you can't be all you were created to be with one parent.*

★★★ *Stop using the phrase, "If it wasn't for you, I could have _____."*

★★★ *Start saying, "Because of you, I have turned it around!"*

★★★ *Use all that built up hurt of not having a perfect parent for your benefit. Do something about it in your own life. Get over it before it destroys you!*

★★★ *Our choices are still our choices, regardless. That being said, not everyone is equipped for the job of being a nurturing parent. They may know what a nurturing parent is and want to be one, but don't actually know how to be one. Maybe, they simply need to be taught.*

Scars to Stars

- ★★★ *Suggestions by others will make you stumble or fall. Use your own cognition and let the decision be your own.*

- ★★★ *Walk in newness, not forgetting but remembering what has helped you along the way.*

- ★★★ *All the things that had your life scarred so deeply have now been revealed and can no longer keep you bound.*

- ★★★ *Yeah, you may have told the story of not having a father figure in your home; or maybe you didn't have a loving mother. You tell how you only had one parent in your life. Your story could be true in the natural, but it doesn't have to stay that way. That's bondage and a stronghold the enemy has placed to set you up. Remember, it still took both parents for you to even exist, no matter what role each played. Now you know, if it wasn't for them, you wouldn't even be here scarred. Use it for your benefit. Yes, that's another deep one, but it's so very true! If it wasn't for parents, children wouldn't have life, for God uses parents to bring forth life. There will always be something we all will have to give an account for; whether we do or did our part, even if it is what you consider a small part that God gave the person to do! If making sure you were born was the only part that your parents were given; be grateful. You're here. Ask God to allow you to use those scars you developed and turn them into special stars so that you can live a productive life and move past the pain of the what-ifs. Every parent was not given the same job. Each parent is an individual person, all different, like you and me. So do your best with what you're given and make sure you do each of your parts in life! As the saying goes, "Misery loves company!" Make the quality decision to let God lead you. Let go and let God, so you can live freely!*

8
Restoration Then *Salvation*

So many different angles showed that restoration was all over my life now. A supernatural experience had taken place on all levels. First and foremost, my relationship with God was renewed. The broken parts of my life, from past hurts and disappointments, were being shot down slowly. One by one. This was an amazing transformation!

I awoke to the sound of gospel music playing and noisy kids in the background. It must be a Sunday. My daughter was playing my favorite song as my son ran around the house dancing and screaming. The sound was so touching. *After all I had been through!* When life has dealt you some crazy hands, you enjoy all the sweet sounds you can when they come with a smile. "Yes, what may I do for you two?", is all I could say as I prepared our Sunday dinner before going to church. Glad to know they both wanted cereal!

Those are the days I hold onto dearly. I enjoyed every single moment, as much as I could. Time with them, was time well spent. It's like saving a piece of your favorite treat; you just don't want it to end, so you hold on to it wrapped up tightly and very close to you. As I began to hold onto all those special memories of my kids growing up, I now realize it was at those moments, God had begun a work of restoring the motherly love and feelings the enemy was slowly trying to sift away from me. Every waking morning was a delight. Some of the days were a little more intense than others but I was still grateful for them, and we made it through.

Regaining is always a delightful feeling. Yes, I can now walk and enjoy the gifts given within the gift of life. True restoration brings appreciation of where you are and where you have come from. All the summers, all the long nights, and all the long days really were life's changing moments.

Even when you feel you're at your lowest point in life, just as the wind begins to blow, know that it's God shifting your life right before your eyes. The wind is a sign and evidence that goodness is in route; evidence of things that are unseen.

Walking on the beach on a hot sunny day, we think *where's the breeze?* Just in that moment, the breeze comes. That's just like those special times in life when things get difficult, and the wind blows a blessing your way. Consider it reassurance that some way, somehow, if the unseen wind can change the atmosphere, then trust in God will change any situation that we can't.

At this moment, begin to stand up and take back things that were taken from you. Allow the deep bitterness and stronghold to be unleashed as your weapon to contend for your life. Fight back against all the things that have wounded you or beaten you in life. You are victorious, even when the adversary works through people you thought loved and cared for you.

Scars that are not given proper treatment and time to heal are still sore when the bandages are pulled off. I'm tired of keeping mine covered up. The wounds can show, however, they shall no more represent sorrow, but they will represent the story of my great tomorrow. Yes, I've made it past the scabs and underneath all the pain, some don't look so bad after being dealt with. Others are just a reminder of what brought me over.

Know, what doesn't kill you, will make you stronger. I'm in my stronger mode! My hands are lifted up high and I have a smile on my face. Giving thanks to God. Not only am I better and stronger but I'm so much wiser. Wiser to know that I can, you can, she can, and he can! We can! Restore, reclaim, rebuild, and rejoice! Yes, a change has come.

While visiting a local church with a friend, you're feeling great about yourself. Not only is the stress dwindling away by the day, shucks, you've lost weight, have a new hairdo, and a new attitude.

As you sit in the service, the familiar words you've always heard growing up in the church have become so, so real at this point in your life.

One particularly stands out. You heard the preacher ask, "Who needs salvation? If you need salvation just come! God will take you in and sup with you (see Revelations 3:20). He will come into your heart and guide you to be used as His servant.

Now you're sitting there having your own conversation after hearing those words in your mind thinking, is He talking to me? Who are You? What is it that You want from me?

So, you say, "Come, You can save me! Save me from what? Can You really save a sinner like me? Do You know how I kept all that hate in my heart because of how others treated me? You still think I'm worth it? People lied to me for no reason, cheated on me for no reason, cursed me because I wasn't like them, and I hated them for that! And You still want someone like me? What about when I lied to others, and no one knew it was me? Can You use a liar? Even if, I wanted to do bodily harm to someone and at times acted on it? What about when I wanted to kill someone and planned it out, yet I couldn't go through with it? Could someone with such a warped mind still be good in Your sight? I tried to hate my sisters and brothers because they mistreated me. Do You still want me?"

The mercy and grace of God is beyond human reasoning. The enemy works within our minds to present scenarios of actions that might cause God to *throw someone back*. But the word of God clearly establishes Jesus' purpose, "For the Son of man is come to seek and to save that which was lost" (Luke 19:10). He did not come to *kick us while we are down* through condemnation, "For God sent not his Son into the world to condemn the world; but that the world through him might be saved" (John 3:17). Too often we meditate on, what the enemy presents as *disqualifiers*, instead of God's infinite mercy, grace, deliverance, and restoration.

> *What about someone who raped and threatened a person and was never caught or punished for it? What about someone who kills an innocent person? Can they too be forgiven? How are they able to come to You after that? Now tell me, who can use someone like that? You keep saying You can.*
>
> *Come on! I'll go a little deeper. What about a woman who gives birth to a child and has other children they treat better because this particular one acts just like their dad. Now how can You want a person like that, while this child wonders why they are treated differently from the other siblings? They have no clue the contributing factor is the mother's anger towards the father. What kind of sense*

does that make? How could that be made good in Your eyes?

What about a person who wakes up to their spouse, knowing they have a significant other on the side? How could You forgive that? Oh yes, that's a hard one! Yet, You say You can handle it. What about when there is a baby involved and the truth is not told about the absent parent and years later it comes out? Now how is that one fixed? The house is torn apart and so is the relationship.

So, You mean to tell me, there's nothing too hard for You? You will forgive all sin and also help each person make it through difficult times in their life? Even when someone feels like they have no one? Now, that's another big one. Wow, You say You're bigger than that? Bigger than we can even imagine?

What do I do about the people who hurt and lied on me at church? Do I keep on being a hypocrite like them? Oh, so You can handle all them too?

Salvation is free for all who will come to Him. Wow! Yes! Yes! Yes! In Matthew, 11th chapter, 28th verse, Jesus says, "Come unto me, all ye that labour and are heavy laden, and I will give you rest."

See, I heard that before, yet I didn't understand what it meant until now. Jesus was saying, if I would have only trusted Him, some of *these things* I had endured, I would not have gone through. Nevertheless, there's no better time like the present!

> Trust in the Lord with all thine heart; and lean not unto thine own understanding. In all thy ways acknowledge him, and he shall direct thy paths.
>
> Proverbs 3:5-6

As the voice went away in my head, I was glad to have been in the service. The next day, I was thinking at a different level. *I need God and He already paid the price for me, so why should I not give my life to Him?* So, I did that very moment and as I began to ask God to come into my life, I was overwhelmed with great joy.

Thanks be to God; bad times don't last always. The rainbow has come again and there will be sunshine. I'm taking it step by step, minute by minute, second by second, every day.

Blinking only for a moment, this maze is slowly coming to an end. I've discovered the right turns and avoided most of the dead ends. The adventure of the hunt for my soul was defeated through salvation. *Yes, I'm overcoming the obstacles that were set before me.*

A word of wisdom gained from experience, when you are faced with something new, make sure you are well equipped for the newness that it will bring. Get all the facts before you even take the first step. Remember to have a shield on standby when you are backed against the wall.

> Put on the whole armour of God, that ye may be able to stand against the wiles of the devil.
> Ephesians 6:11

Being prepared always helps, even with every unexpected task.

Maze, oh maze, you weren't made with paths just of quick turns, but yet you exist for those with willingness to take the journey. Far away you seem impossible to take on for a challenge, but up close and in person, I win!

Rekindled not just for a brief moment, resting in the bosom of the Almighty, just as a mother or father holds their newborn, You rock me in the cradle of Your arms. Blinking and blocking out the voice of dismay.

Behold I stand at the door of your heart knocking. How could you make me feel so unwanted? How could you make me feel that my gift of love and nurturing to you is like an old dirty rag, used only to clean up messes and spills, to later be thrown into the trash?

Scars to Stars

What God has restored unto me, how dare you come and try and interfere. Opening up the wounds of familiar hurts and disappointments, I take charge over thee, thy enemy, that tries to come up through you.

It's refreshing to know that the scars of worthlessness are no longer scars that I can't look at or cry about. I can uncover and remove the bandage and see the healing even from afar. For once in a lifetime this is just a thing of my past.

Yes, God has restored unto me a clean heart and renewed unto me a righteous spirit. Now walking from this dreary day, I am able to recognize what I have. Knowing, I am more of a believer through Christ who strengthens me (*see* Philippians 4:13).

As I backed up and have taken control of that which had me captive, I realized all I had to do was look up, let go, and let God! Thank You!

Now you know revealed SCARS show that you have been healed. You made it. No matter the struggle or the storm, they are there to remind you of a difficult time in life that you have conquered.

Take the bandage off and allow those scars to heal. Remember you are who you are because of those same scars.

I say to you, "I made it!"

I say to God, "I am what I am because of who You are!

From now on, don't let anyone trouble me with these things. For I bear on my body the scars that show I belong to Jesus.
        Galatians 6:17, NLT

Thank You Lord, for turning my SCARS into STARS!

Spiritual

Transition & Timing

Admiration

Reputation

Self-worth

Thank You for My Joy!

Special Thanks

Thank you, Deborah Williams for being my best friend for over 30 years and being there through the good times and the not so good times. You were my sounding board in so many ways and yet you didn't judge me. Thank you for lending me your shoulder, holding my hand, and wiping away many tears. Most importantly, thank you for the laughs and fun times we shared.

Stella Portlock (Rest in Peace); for imparting her wisdom and beauty into my life! Helping me find my inner beauty! She is forever in my heart and God rest her soul. She was always trying to help me stay focused in difficult situations! All smiles for the lip liner & lip gloss.

Mary McCullough; for always helping Mrs. Stella stay on me in and out of the nail shop, when life was crazy all around me. Showing me the same love and reminding me I could and would be okay if I held onto God's hand.

Mrs. Emma Murry, Oh God, words can't express how I'm so grateful for all the laughs and talks we had. The encouragement you gave me on a day-to-day basis; even when you said you were proud of my accomplishments in those rough times meant so much. I truly thank you. God did make things alright.

Dedra Haynes-Waller

Thanks to Pastor Ira Lightsey and the St. Mary's Church family of Mims, FL, for all your prayers and kind words for me and my family.

My girls, pals, aces, my God… words can't even begin to say how all of these ladies have been a great part of my life in so many ways: Daphne G. Lamons, Talvia W. Peterson, Monique Rush, Roslyn Murry, April H. Smith, Cynthia R. Render, Princetta B. Clark, Rosalind Martin, Latressa (Tricia) Taylor, Carla Murray, and Tommeyzina Williams. God placed each of you there to be just what I needed and when I needed you. Thank you for every kind word and every part of you that you gave unselfishly to me.

Thank You!
Dedra

Scars to Stars

Thought for Today, Tomorrow, & Forever;
Until You See Yourself Free!

Oh God, free me from this thing that has me bound!
I'm stuck.
My mind needs to be free again.
Please!
Un-stick me!
Un-stick my heart from the hurt, they caused me!
Un-stick my mind so I can forget the wrong that has happened in my life that's caused me to remain in the past!
Help me to move forward from these inward scars that have me living in a state of sorrowfulness.
Allow me to trade in my scars for more stars.
Each one I give back to You.
I need You to get to the root of the things that eat at my soul, I want to be free!
Free to live a life fulfilling unto You.
I give back all my selfishness for Your *Sincerity*.
I trade in my cunning ways just so that Your *Consecration* can bring change in me.
I give back the addictions that had me bound, to obtain *Admiration* through my life.
Oh God, take these repetitive sins and place *Restoration* upon me.
For I need to get rid of these situations that cause so much heartache and pain, for I need Your *Salvation*!

I need to be free!

I was hit,
left alone,
stepped on,
torn down with words of deceit,
raped of my youth,
shoved aside by those I thought loved me.
Help me!
For I need You to show me the real me; whom I'm supposed to be after recovering from all this mess.
Allow me to take all those bricks and build me a firm foundation that I may share with someone else, the greatness of a house that's not made with man's hands.
I thank You in Jesus name.
AMEN!
Free…

About the Author

Thanking God for where He has brought me up to this present time. I am a daughter, sister, friend, auntie, mother, wife, and grandmother. Most importantly, I am a child of the Almighty God! I have two children and a total of six children by marriage.

I love singing, my family time, and worshipping God. By God's grace, He has allowed me to record my first gospel demo titled, *Just Me, Dedra*. Songs include, *I Am What I Am, My Knees are Weak, and Thank You*. They were recorded at Demo-Ville Recording Studios in Titusville, FL, in April, June, and August of 2012.

I've been a nail technician since 1995 and I currently work at the Brevard Property Appraisers Office.

I am a member of the Love Center Church in Titusville, FL. I newly accepted the call of the Gift of Prophecy and received a certificate of completion June 23rd of 2012 from the School of Prophets under the leadership of Apostle Janet C. Moragne, Soaring Eagle Ministries, in Cocoa, FL.

With the help of the Lord, I'm always seeking what is ever in His will for my life. I say to all, trust in the Lord. If He did it for me, surely He can do the same for you!

★★★

Most important of all, continue to show deep love for each other, for love covers a multitude of sins.
1 Peter 4:8, NLT

www.ingramcontent.com/pod-product-compliance
Lightning Source LLC
Chambersburg PA
CBHW071154090426
42736CB00012B/2334